The Pregnant Pen

The Expectant Mother's Guide to Baby Showers and Thank You Notes

Diane Quast

Published by Big Belly Enterprises
P.O. Box 4004, Redondo Beach, CA 90277
(310) 251-8636

Manufactured in the United States of America
10 9 8 7 6 5 4 3 2

Credits
Cover design and illustrations by Anthony Torres, T1 Creative
Inside art and graphics by Paul Quast
Design assistance by Theresa Quast
Editor, Heather Szott, Hawkeye Editing

Library of Congress Control Number: 2005909738
1. Baby Shower Planning & Etiquette. 2. Thank You Notes.

ISBN 0-9771525-1-0

To my family

Table of Contents

all: 698-8400

Baby Shower Decorations

Here is a quick decorating idea for a baby shower. Cover the tables with paper or plastic table coverings. If the tables are rectangular, make baby footprints down the center using the edge of your fist for the foot and fingers for the toes with ink or acrylic craft paint. Round or square tables can have the footprints scattered randomly, or the table can be outlined in the footprints. Streamers, ribbons, or confetti in coordinating colors provide the finishing touch. Another alternative to the confetti could be candy or baby items to match the color scheme. One bottle of craft paint is more than enough for all of the tables. This idea offers that personal touch along with a money-saving bonus. — CW

Pennysaver - March 27, 2008

24618295B813

www.llpen

—————

Chapter One

Being a Gracious Guest of Honor

When family, friends and co-workers ask to host a shower in your honor, it's a lovely testament to your friendships. Showers and other gift-giving opportunities are not an expected event during everyone's pregnancy, thus when a friend offers to host a shower, your role is to be as gracious as possible. This book is intended to provide the mother-to-be with the insight to fulfill her role with poise.

This chapter provides valuable information to ensure you handle yourself tactfully, and it identifies what your host(s) and guests expect from you before, during, and after your baby shower.

When a Friend Asks to Host a Shower in Your Honor

Your role begins early in the shower's planning stages. Your first job is to provide your host with a comprehensive invitation list. Before you compile the list, chat with your host(s) to find out if there are space limitations that will restrict the number of guests. With these restrictions in mind, create a list of appropriate guests, including family, friends and close co-workers. Providing the list and number of anticipated guests as early as possible helps your host(s) determine the location of your party and enables them to establish a budget for the invitations, food and decorations.

Be sure your invitation list includes the first and last names of all your guests, their mailing address, phone numbers and e-mail addresses to make following up easy with guests who have not responded to the invitation. On average, invitations will be mailed four to six weeks prior to the event, so it's crucial you give the host(s) the guest list about three months before the event's date.

Note: Don't forget to send invitations to far-away family and friends. They'll be delighted to be included and will often send their blessings and a gift in their absence.

Coordinating Multiple Showers

In the event you are invited to have more than one shower, it's important to manage your guest lists to ensure multiple invitations are not sent to the same people. A friend should not receive more than one invitation to a shower, as it may suggest that she bring a gift to each shower. However, if you have a close friend that you would like to attend all of your showers, be sure to tell her to expect the invitations, but that a gift at each shower is not necessary.

If you're not sure which party to invite a friend to, consider inviting her to the party at which she'll know the most people or is apt to make the most new friends. That way, she's sure to have plenty of people to talk to and sit with at mealtime.

A Shower for Your Second Child

It's becoming more common for friends to throw smaller and more quaint second showers, and it's up to you to decide if you'd like to have the party. While some moms feel awkward about a second shower, many moms appreciate the attention the new baby is receiving. The invitation list for the second shower usually will include close family and friends. Also, if you find that you need or want specific items for your second child, it's appropriate to let people know where you are registered.

Registering for Gifts

Modern tradition allows for the soon-to-be parents to register at one or more baby stores for items they want to receive. Many gift givers appreciate buying from registries, as it takes the guesswork out of selecting items that the new parents need.

After completing your invitation list, it's time to visit your local baby store and register for gifts. Many baby stores have a formal registry process that includes a packet containing registry cards you can include with the invitations. It's appropriate and expected to let your guests know where you have registered, and this information may also be printed on the actual shower invitation. Including registry information saves people time and is appreciated, especially for far-away guests.

After you register, be sure to manage your registry on-line or visit the store to ensure you have enough items and at varying costs, even after the shower has occurred. Many new moms receive gifts after the baby is born and having an available registry ensures that you continue to receive gifts you want and need.

Planning the Party

The host(s) of your shower should include you in the party planning process, including selecting the date for the event. The shower should be held between the sixth and eighth month of your pregnancy, which ensures that you have a belly to show off without the threat of going into labor.

Your host will probably ask for your feedback on some party details, but it's important to allow your host(s) to coordinate the theme, invitations and games. It's also appropriate to give her feedback along the way to assist her in planning a party that fits your personality. If you want to assist in the party planning, volunteer your time by helping to prepare the shower invitations or make party favors with your host(s). Also, do not insist on paying for anything. Allow your host(s) to pay for the shower, to the extent they can, and accept the shower as one would a gift.

The Day of the Shower

Arrive at the shower early to welcome your guests. Often, your host(s) will be finalizing last-minute details, so your help in welcoming guests and getting them situated is appreciated. Also, if you feel up to it, plan to stay late and be one of the last guests to leave. In addition to hanging out with your friends and chatting about all the great presents you received, you'll have the opportunity to thank all your guests for coming to the shower and for their great gifts. You are not expected to help clean, but offer to help where you can. Having your husband drop by near the end of the shower is a great way for your guests to congratulate the father-to-be. Plus, he can be very helpful in loading all your gifts into the car.

Be sure to have fun and enjoy the moment. The shower is all about you, and your family and friends want to see you enjoy yourself.

Maintaining a List of Your Baby Shower Gifts

Ideally, one of your friends at the shower will maintain a detailed list of your gifts with each giver's name. If not, you'll need to create your gift list after you've brought home the goodies. As you unpack the items from their boxes, jot down the name of the gift giver from the gift card along with a description of the gift, so you can write your notes from a complete list. A sample list is included at the end of this book. Your list is also a fun item to include in baby's first-year book. Be sure to keep all the cards, too! Warm, heartfelt sentiments are often the most precious part of the gift. When baby grows up, she, too, will enjoy reading what mommy's friends had to say.

After the Shower

Thank you notes should be sent within a couple of weeks of receiving gifts. This includes sending notes to all the guests who brought gifts to your shower, each friend who contributed toward a group gift, far-away loved ones who mailed their presents to you, and the host(s) of your shower if they gave you a gift at the party. Thank you notes are important, because they let people know you received the gift, especially if it was sent. The note also lets the gift giver know you and your spouse appreciate their gift and that it will be put to good use. Finally, taking the time to write a note reassures the gift giver that you value their friendship and appreciate the time and money they put into choosing a gift for your baby and coming to your shower.

Note: A late thank you note is better than no note at all.

Chapter Two

Getting Started

Congratulations! You're on your way to a new chapter in your life and the most important job of your life – motherhood. In anticipation of your new arrival, a baby shower has been thrown in your honor, and now it is time to write notes thanking all the special people who made it a day you'll always remember.

This chapter contains information on selecting stationery and how to get started writing your notes. It breaks the note down into four sections, making it easy to distinguish and develop creative notes for each gift you receive. Thank you notes are intended to be brief and should simply thank the gift giver for their gift. Do not feel as though you need to write more to fill up space on the stationery.

The Note

Once you have your gift list, it's time to start writing thank you notes. A nicely written thank you note that appropriately acknowledges the gift will make the gift giver happy to have been a part of your celebration.

The Stationery

There are many manufacturers of cute baby shower thank you notes. You may also decide to order personalized note cards that match the original shower invitation. Either way, choose a card that does not have a preprinted sentiment, so you have the space to fully express thanks in your own words. Also, many couples have monogrammed note cards left over from their weddings and using them to acknowledge baby gifts is an appropriate and excellent way to use them up.

As with a letter, there are four parts to every note: the greeting, the body, the closing, and the signature.

The Greeting

The greeting begins the note, and usually means "hello." A customary opening simply uses the word dear, such as, "Dear Sue," but the note should be addressed according to your familiarity with the individual. If you do not know the person's last name, or are unsure how to spell it, do your homework. Contact the host and other friends to find out a correct name or spelling. Also, if the note came signed by an entire family, it's appropriate to write the note to the mother and include the rest of the family in the body of the note. An example would be, "Dear Mrs. Jones, I would like to thank you and your family for the lovely baby gift."

The Body

The body of the note is a brief paragraph of three or four sentences, expressing thanks for the gift. Always mention the item by name. If you're not sure what it is, describe it. You might also think about including a description of how you plan to use or display the gift. If you received a basket filled with multiple items, you only need to identify a couple of the larger items. If it was a basket filled with similar or themed items, you can thank the gift giver for their basket of useful supplies, then describe how you intend to put one or two of the items to use.

It's optional to include a statement referring to your registry. For example, "Thanks for taking the time to look at our registry and for picking out something we really need." On the other hand, it's inappropriate to send a generic note for the gift from your registry or to include only your signature on a card that contains a preprinted sentiment, such as "Thanks for the baby gift."

Be sure to end the paragraph with a final thank you. And remember, the next time you see or talk to the gift giver, be sure to thank her again!

The Closing

The closing ends the note and says "good-bye" to the reader. It always precedes your signature. How you choose to close a note depends on your relationship with the individual, not on the expense of the gift. Some examples are Love, Sincerely, Warmly, Fondly and Gratefully.

The Signature

The signature lets the reader know who wrote the note. Traditionally, it's the mother-to-be who writes and signs all the notes. Thus, you should sign the notes according to how people know you. If the gift givers are family, friends or co-workers, your first name is all that is needed. Include your husband's name if the gift came from his family, friends or co-workers. In the event you had a couple's shower or the gift was addressed to both of you, you may decide to sign the note with both your names. Finally, if you are thanking a child who calls you by your married name, it's appropriate to sign the note using only your last name, such as, "Mrs. Smith."

Chapter Three

Sample Notes for Baby Shower Gifts

Unless your baby shower was held three months before your due date, you may not have the time or inclination to sit quietly and focus on writing creative notes for all the gifts you received. More likely, writing your thank you notes is one more thing that needs to get done before baby's arrival. To alleviate the stress of writing thank you notes, this chapter provides more than 80 sample notes for most items you are sure to receive before and after the baby arrives.

These notes were written to address many gift-giving scenarios, including baby showers, couples' showers, gifts for twins, adopted children, unexpected visits from friends bringing gifts, and more. While each note is unique, they follow the same pattern: they express thanks for the gift, include an identifying or describing sentence, and include a statement on how the gift will be used. Each note contains one final thank you before the closing sentiment.

In the event you receive a unique item not included in this book, you now have the tools to create your own personalized note that appropriately acknowledges your gift giver and makes them happy to have been a part of your celebration.

Accepting Gifts for Your Twins

One of the big differences when thanking your family and friends for their gifts for your twins is that they may have given you double or triple the gifts. When writing your notes, acknowledge the gifts on behalf of the twins, the babies, or use the babies' names if you're ready to share that information. Be sure to include a statement on how you or the babies intend to use the items. When closing the note, be sure to thank the gift giver again for their generous gifts.

Accepting Gifts for Your Adopted Child

There are many scenarios that precede a successful adoption, and etiquette may guide you to keep that information private or shared only with those closest to you.

Baby showers and visits from family and friends bearing gifts generally occur after you share news of your adoption. When writing your notes, do not feel obligated to explain the adoption. The gift giver already knows that your adoption was successful; now they want to know that you received their present and will put it to good use. Save the personal information for visits and phone calls with loved ones.

Note: If you're not ready to share the gender of your baby or the name you've selected, it's appropriate to simply refer to "baby" in your notes.

Following are sample thank you notes.

Art Work

Dear Ariana,

Thank you so much for the original Wyland painting you, Michelle, and Lisa picked out for the baby. It is absolutely amazing and will be perfect in the nursery. It was extremely thoughtful of the three of you to pick out something so unique and priceless. Thanks again for your thoughtful and generous gift.

Love,

Kiara

Baby Gate

Dear Amy,

Thank you for coming to my shower and for the sliding baby gate. I read the directions, and it seems like it will be easy to use even when I have the baby in my arms. Thanks again for sharing in my special day and for the thoughtful gift.

Fondly,

Jen

Baby Proofing Items

Dear Uncle Jim,

Thanks for the handy gift of baby-proofing items. It's hard to believe that we'll need so much, and we're thankful to you for getting us started on creating a safe place for baby. We're definitely going to need your help deciding what needs to be installed now and what can wait. Maybe you can join us for dinner one night soon and help get us started.

Thanks again,

Penny and Jim

Backpack Carrier

Dear Jesse,

Thank you for coming to my baby shower and especially for the awesome backpack carrier. John and I have been talking about taking the baby on hikes, and the carrier will be just perfect. It's so lightweight that hiking with baby should be a breeze! Thanks again for being so thoughtful – you can be sure we'll put your gift to good use!

Gratefully,

Barbara and John

Baskets

Dear Beth,

What a great gift! I received so many clothes and toys at the shower, but I really didn't think about where I'd put everything. The lovely lined baskets will be the perfect place to stack diapers, toys, clothes, and so much more! Thanks for thinking outside the basket for such a handy and pretty present.

Warmly,

Teresa

Bassinet

Dear Marie,

Thank you so much for the lovely white lace bassinet for the baby. I love the extra features like the timed rocking and the lullaby music. Having the baby sleep next to our bed will provide us with an extra moment of peace in the middle of the night. I just wasn't prepared to have his bed be so much nicer than ours! Warmest thanks for such a lovely and generous gift.

Love,

Marguerite

Bath Supplies

Dear Melanie,

It was very thoughtful of you to think of us and send the box of washcloths, bubble bath, and water toys for our new arrival. Thanks to your complete bath ensemble, we're sure to have the cleanest baby in town. All my thanks.

Warmly,

Nicole

Bathtub

Dear Betty,

I was delighted to receive the infant bathtub and the variety of water toys. I'm a little nervous about bath time, but your gift will make bathing much easier and fun. Because of you, little Brenda is going to be the best smelling baby in town! Thanks for coming to my shower and for sharing in our excitement.

Fondly,

Donna

Bedding Sets

Dear Jill,

The baby animal quilt and matching accessories are absolutely adorable. We looked at so many different prints before we agreed on this pattern. The baby's room is almost finished; the only thing we need now is the baby! Thank you for your comfy and generous gift.

Warmly,

Delia

Blankets (hand knit)

Dear Grandma,

We were very touched to receive the beautiful blankets you made for the twins. They are absolutely lovely, and I can't begin to imagine how long it must have taken to knit them. It was quite creative of you to use the same pattern on both blankets but to reverse the colors. Again, thank you so much for your precious gift and for keeping us in your thoughts during this very exciting time.

All our love,

Tina and Tony

Books

Dear Holly,

Thanks again for the wonderful children's books. I can't wait for the baby to arrive, so I can share my love of books with her. I especially liked the children's prayer book. I know it will become a family ritual to read from it every night. Thanks again for the perfect gift.

Warmly,

Anne

Booster Seat

Dear Jean,

I was delighted to receive the portable booster seat and the baby food for our new arrival. They will come in very handy when we go to the lake and on camping trips this summer. Thanks for your very thoughtful gift and for sharing in my special day!

Warmly,

Jessica

Bottle Sterilizer

Dear Laura,

I really appreciated receiving the bottle sterilizer as a gift for our new baby. I know it's going to be a true time saver, since I've heard I'll be going through about eight bottles a day. With that in mind, I have a feeling the sterilizer will be working all day! Many thanks for the timely gift.

Gratefully,

Julia

Bottle Warmer

Dear Lisa,

Thank you so much for keeping us in your thoughts as we completed the adoption of our little Rita. We are so fortunate to have her in our lives and can't wait to introduce her to you. Thanks, too, for the thoughtful gift. The bottle warmer is perfect and will ensure that her milk will always be the right temperature. Many thanks again for the quick warm-up.

Sincerely,

Dana

Bottles

Dear Anne,

Thank you so much for the baby bottles. You can be sure I'm going to put Ron to work now – especially for those midnight feedings! It was also very nice to include the bottle brush and dishwasher baskets to help keep everything nice and clean. Thanks again for your thoughtful gift.

Fondly,

Bridget

Bottles (twins/adoption)

Dear Laura,

Thank you so much for the baby bottles. It has been extremely helpful to have so many, since Mike and I are working double time with the feedings. We really appreciate your thoughtful gift and for helping us welcome our new babies, Ben and Joey, into our family.

Fondly,

Bridget

Bouncer

Dear John and Dorothy,

I just wanted to send a quick note of thanks to let you know the baby bouncer arrived today. It is a generous gift and something that I anticipate will get lots of use. For one, it's sure to become a favorite place for baby to play while I prepare (or eat) dinner! Thanks again for your thoughtful and fun present.

Love,

Lara and Luke

Bouncy Seat

Dear Kaylee,

Apparently, good news travels fast. I can't believe you already heard that our baby came a few weeks early! It was thoughtful and generous of you to send the bouncy seat. With its little seat belt, it has already been a great place for little Sue to sit while I take a quick shower! I'll be sure to email pictures, but I do hope a visit with us is in your future.

Love,

Heather

Breast Pump

Dear Sandi,

It was extremely generous of you, Linda, and Mary to give me a breast pump in anticipation of my returning to work. I'm sure the baby will appreciate the fresh milk, and I plan to put Walt to work and have him feed the baby in the middle of the night. Thanks again for your very generous gift and for being so supportive.

Love,

Jessica

Burp Cloths (handmade)

Dear Emily,

I was so delighted to receive your handmade burp cloths. They're absolutely beautiful, and I'm going to find it very difficult to use them for their intended purpose! Your creativity never ceases to amaze me. When baby is older, we'll have to get together and find a way to turn your hobbies into a business. Thanks again for taking the time to make something so practical and personal.

Fondly,

Lilly

Car Seat

Dear Mom,

It's hard to believe that we'll soon be chauffeuring our baby in the infant car seat you gave to us. With our due date just around the corner, we'll be putting it to use very soon bringing Caitlin home from the hospital. Thank you for the generous gift and for everything else you've given us. We love and appreciate you very much.

Love,

Kate and Fred

Care Package

Dear Kathleen,

What a surprise it was to receive your care package filled with items for our new babies, Kendra and Kelly. Apparently good news travels fast, because I still have to send out their birth announcements. It was extremely thoughtful of you to think of us, and to send so many things – you can be sure everything will be put to good use. Many thanks again.

Sincerely,

Jenna

Carrier

Dear Betty,

Thank you for coming to my baby shower and for the wonderful gifts. The baby carriers are the perfect gift for Michael and me, as we plan to continue our active lives, even with the twins. We'll now be able to keep Mindy and Matthew close by when we go on walks and hikes – even to the mall. Thank you for being so thoughtful and generous and for helping us welcome the twins into our lives.

Love,

Lucy and Michael

CD Player

Dear Michelle,

What a cool gift! Baby Nicho will be going to bed every night listening to some mellow tunes, and I'm sure before we know it, he'll be swapping out the CDs to play some hip-hop. The CD player is Jim's favorite present and is already fixed to the crib. Many thanks again for coming to my shower and for sharing in my special day.

Fondly,

Lindy

Changing Pad & Cover

Dear Frank,

Thank you so much for the changing pad and the yellow and green pad covers. We appreciate you looking on our registry to pick out a gift for little Joey. I've heard that I can plan to change 5,000 diapers by the time our baby turns three, so you can be very sure we'll put your gift to good use! Again, thanks for thinking of us and our little one on the way.

Regards,

Tim and Tina

Changing Table

Dear Richard,

The changing table you sent to us is now the best piece of furniture we own. I hope Ben won't mind having his diaper changed in the living room! Actually, it'll be in his room, and it is perfect since it has so much storage for his clothes, diapers and lotions. Thanks for picking out something so nice for your new nephew.

Fondly,

Lara and Rich

Cloth Diapers

Dear Melissa,

I can't thank you enough for all the cotton diapers. I plan to have one embroidered with the baby's name for a keepsake. It was also extremely generous of you to sign us up for a year of diaper service. I didn't know this service still existed! Thanks again for being so thoughtful.

Warm regards,

Nancy

Clothes (boy)

Dear April,

Thank you so much for the baby gift! You've absolutely spoiled Ryan with the three little outfits and pair of tennis shoes. The clothes are all so cute, but I especially love the blue jean jacket embroidered with the little tiger. It'll be perfect for our cool fall weather and is sure to keep him warm and in style. Thanks again for helping Ryan gain the title of best-dressed boy on the block!

With love,

Camilla

Clothes (girl)

Dear Lisa,

The little red and white-checkered jumper, matching hat and shoes are absolutely adorable. Thank you for picking out such a cute outfit for Susan. With your fashion influence, she's definitely going to be the best-dressed baby at the lake this year! Many thanks again.

Warmly,

Trish

Clothes (twins)

Dear Anna,

Thank you very much for the little outfits for our new babies, David and Traci. It was extremely generous of you to pick out so many – I think you've outfitted them for the next few months! We are very blessed to have the twins in our lives, and can't wait for you to meet them. Many thanks again.

Warmly,

Tammy

Cradle Swing

Dear Georgia,

We were delighted to receive the cradle swing in anticipation of our new arrival. It has some pretty spectacular features with the lighted mobile and the little fish and sea creatures swinging above. I know it will be a favorite resting spot for the baby. It was a lot of fun to have a couple's shower, and we were so happy you and Terry were able to make it! Thanks again for your thoughtful and generous gift.

Warmly,

Danni

Crib

Dear Aunt Trisha and Uncle Frank,

When you told us to keep an eye out for a special delivery, I was expecting a letter. We were so surprised to receive the beautiful maple crib you sent for our new baby. In such a lovely new bed, little Robert will be sleeping like a baby through the night. Thank you so much for your extremely generous present and for helping us welcome our new baby into our lives.

Love,

Linda and Tom

Crib Bumpers

Dear Felicia,

Thank you for the crib bumpers for Amelia's bed. Apparently, you found out that the baby store no longer sells the bumpers we registered for, and I appreciate you taking the time to find a pattern that matches her bedding. The sage green color really is pretty, and I know the padding will protect her when she rolls into the side of the crib. Thanks for keeping an eye out for the perfect gift.

Gratefully,

Janice

Crib - Portable Travel Crib

Dear Theresa,

The green and blue travel crib you picked out for our new baby is even cuter than you had described. It has so many neat attachments; I don't think the baby will ever want to come out of it! I know we're going to get a lot of use from it when we travel this summer, and I'm sure to use it as a play yard when baby gets a little older. Thanks so much for your thoughtful and very useful gift.

All my love,

Alyson

Crib Sheets

Dear Stephanie,

Timothy's early arrival has thrown off my thank you note schedule, but before any more time passes… thank you for the two sets of fitted crib sheets. The flannel sheet is sure to keep him nice and warm in the winter, while we plan to use the combed cotton sheet to keep him cool in the summer. Thanks again for a gift we'll be using all year!

Sincerely,

Barbara

Diaper Bag

Dear Tracy,

I really appreciated receiving your baby shower gift. It was extremely generous of you to fill the deluxe diaper bag with all the essentials, and I feel ready to leave the house with my bag filled with pacifiers, diaper cream, sippy cups, first aide ointment, and everything else! Thanks again for such a thoughtful and useful gift.

Love,

Dawn

Diaper Trashcan

Dear Karen,

Thank goodness someone invented a trashcan for stinky diapers. And thank you for filling it with clean diapers and making it a present to Josh and me. You can be sure we'll be putting your gift to good use for the next few years! Who would have known I'd be sending out a thank you note for a trashcan, but I mean it when I say thank you.

Warmly,

Lois

Diapers

Dear Bella,

Thank you very much for the box of diapers for our new baby, Jason. It was extremely thoughtful of you to think of us, and to drop off something so needed. We're extremely grateful to have you as our neighbor and really appreciate you dropping by for the quick visit. Many thanks again.

Gratefully,

Rebecca and Jim

Diapers

Dear Bridget,

Thanks for dropping by the other day and for all the diapers. It's hard to believe our babies will be using so many – it seems like I'll be on diaper duty for years. I really appreciated you taking the time from your busy schedule for a quick visit, and I hope you'll be able to do it again when we have more time to chat. Many thanks again for your thoughtful gift and warm wishes as Mike and I get into the hang of parenting twins!

Gratefully,

Rebecca

DVD's/Videos

Dear Lulu,

Thank you so much for sending the fun and interactive DVDs for the baby. I've been hearing some great things about this series, and now I won't feel so guilty putting on a DVD, because the baby will be learning her ABCs. Tom and I really appreciated your loving words in your card, and we're very grateful to have you as a friend. Thanks again for thinking of us.

With love,

Rachel

Formula

Dear Jenny,

Thank you for getting us started with the four cans of formula for baby. I still can't believe she'll consume about a can a week! I guess you'll always know where I am – either feeding the baby or washing bottles! Baby, too, thanks you in advance for the yummy present.

Warmly,

Terri

Frames

Dear Brooke,

It was extremely sweet of you to pick out such a cute frame set for our baby's pictures. The matt that came preprinted with newborn, six months, and one-year is such a great idea that once those pictures are taken, we plan to hang them on the wall by her bedroom door for everyone to see. Thanks again for the very thoughtful gift.

Sincerely,

Linda

Gift Basket

Dear Lois,

Sean and I are extremely grateful to you and the staff of the marketing department for all the wonderful baby items. I think this gift will single-handedly fulfill all of baby's needs for the first year! All the clothes, toys, and bath items are great and are going to be put to very good use. Thanks for coordinating such a lovely gift, and please share our thanks with the entire team.

Fondly,

Rebecca

Gift Card

Dear Kimberly,

Thank you so much for your generous gift certificate to the baby store. Jerry and I were there last week and saw several items we still need to feel prepared for baby's arrival. We plan to put your gift card to use and get the daddy diaper bag so that when we're out and about, we'll have everything we need in one fashionable place. Thanks again for your thoughtful gift and the kind words in your note.

Love,

Beth

Hamper

Dear Mary,

Although I hate doing laundry, I was very excited to receive your lovely folding green hamper. I hadn't thought about what we'd use to collect Sally's dirty clothes, and you've solved our dilemma with a fashionable hamper. Thanks for thinking outside the basket!

Sincerely,

Joanna

Handmade Gift

Dear Elizabeth,

The nameplate you made for little Roscoe out of seashells and driftwood is amazing. I can't believe you took the time to search the beach for the perfect shells to spell out his name. Thank you for taking the time to make such a lovely and personal gift!

All my love,

Kari

Healthcare Items

Dear Mrs. Messing,

It was very thoughtful of you to send the basket full of healthcare essentials for our new baby. I was planning to prepare a list of everything I should have handy in case of an emergency, but you've done it for us. Thanks for being so thoughtful and generous.

Sincerely,

Karla

High Chair

Dear Kathy,

I know I thanked you at the baby shower for baby's highchair, but I wanted to thank you again and let you know that it was delivered to our home today. The little clip-on animals are very cute and will be two less things for baby to throw off the tray. Even though it will be a little while before we use it, we really appreciate your thoughtfulness.

Warmly,

Martha

Humidifier

Dear Theresa,

It was very thoughtful of you to give us a humidifier for our new baby. I've heard that humidifiers are great for putting moisture back in the air during winter months when the heater is on. Thanks for keeping the baby's best interests at heart and for your generous gift.

Sincerely,

Frances

Jogging Stroller

Dear Anne Marie,

You were extremely generous to give us a jogging stroller for a baby gift. Thank you for thinking of us and for giving me a little motivation to help me lose the baby weight. When Emily is old enough to ride in it, would you like to join us for a jog around the high school track? Your kindness and motivation are very much appreciated.

Warmly,

Bernadette

Jumper

Dear Uncle Richard,

I would have known it was you who gave us the baby jumper, even had you forgotten to enclose a card with your gift. Who else would be thinking about how to develop baby's vertical jump so soon? The jumper is great, and it will fit perfectly in our bedroom doorframe. I'm looking forward to watching her jump around, burn a little energy and, yes, be the captain of her future volleyball team. Thanks again.

Love,

Sandy

Keepsake

Dear Sherri,

We feel very blessed to have received such a lovely pendant necklace for the baby. The little angel engraving is so beautiful and ornate, I know it will become a family heirloom that will be passed down for many generations. Though you might not see baby wearing it for some time, you can be assured it's in a safe place until the right time to show it off. All our thanks.

Love,

Kate & Will

Mattress

Dear Aunt Nohad,

I just wanted to send a personal thank you note for taking us shopping and for buying the mattress for Jimmy's new crib. We are very lucky to have such a loving and generous family. There's no way we could afford to do everything our family has done for us. Thank you for the fun day and for your most needed gift.

Love,

Lucy

Meal Drop-off

Dear Marguerite,

It was extremely thoughtful of you to prepare my favorite meal and bring it by the other night for our family dinner. Frank especially loved the chocolate cake dessert you picked up. Your home cooked meal was a blessing, as you can imagine I'm not spending much time in the kitchen, and we appreciate you keeping us in your thoughts. Thanks again for the delicious meal!

Love,

Diane

Mobile

Dear Ursula,

Thank you for the fun animal mobile that plays the great tunes. It's amazing that some really wild creatures have been created to entertain our children! I know baby will have fun watching the monkey, toad and bunny whirl above her to Beethoven. Thanks again.

Fondly,

Diane

Monitor (audio)

Dear Francis,

I'm sorry you couldn't make it to my baby shower, but I truly appreciate you dropping off a gift. The baby monitor is absolutely perfect, and I know it will save me many trips to the baby's room to check and see that she's ok. Thanks for being so thoughtful, and I hope we will have another chance to catch up before the baby is born.

With gratitude,

Dolores

Monitor (video)

Dear Michelle,

Thank you for coming to my baby shower and for the video baby monitor. With our multi-level home, I know it will save us many trips running up and down the stairs to check on the baby. We appreciate you taking the time to check our registry for something we really need. Thanks again for your very thoughtful and generous gift.

Gratefully,

Suzie

Music CD

Dear Laney,

Thank you for the Beethoven classical music CD for children. Listening to classical music is supposed to stimulate a baby's brain development, so you can be sure we'll be playing this CD often! Thanks again for the great tunes.

Warmly,

Wanda

Nursing Pillow

Dear Cathleen,

Thank you so much for the support pillow. I've been hearing that this is a must-have for every new mom and that it will be a lifesaver for the next year. It will be fun to see Aaron use it, too, from tummy time to helping him sit up. The race car fabric is absolutely perfect for Aaron's room, and it matches the rocking chair as if it were a set. Thanks again!

Fondly,

Lilly

Personalized Gift

Dear Brooke,

I know I thanked you for the lovely blanket embroidered with Katie's name and birth information when you dropped by, but I love it so much I wanted to thank you again. It is such a thoughtful gift, one I'll treasure for a long time. I can always count on you to surprise me with something so personal. Thanks again.

Warmly,

Penny

Photo Album

Dear Maya,

Thank you so much for the lovely "Little Bear" first year photo album. I'm looking forward to filling it with pictures, and I really like that some of the borders are preprinted with milestone accomplishments. With your help, I'm sure to remember to take all the right pictures! Thanks again for your thoughtful gift.

Sincerely,

Julia

Playmat/Gym (adoption)

Dear Margo,

It's so hard to believe that Bill and I are parents! I wasn't sure the adoption would ever go through, and I am still on cloud nine every time I look at little Tyler. We really appreciate receiving the padded play mat and have already started to give him tummy time using the little string bean pillow that came with it. I can't wait for you to meet our new little boy and hope you can drop by soon. Many thanks.

Love,

Emily

Play Saucer

Dear Stephanie,

Thank you so much for coming to my baby shower and for our new baby's play saucer. It has so many twisting and spinning trinkets on it that baby is sure to get a good workout. I also think it will be a great place for baby while I take a minute for myself! Thanks again for your fun gift.

Warmly,

Lori

Play Yard

Dear Nancy,

I was delighted you could attend my baby shower, and I really appreciate your thoughtful gift. I hadn't thought much about our dog's interactions with baby, but the play yard seems like the perfect solution to keeping the two separated for the time being. I know in a few months, it'll be the dog that'll need protection from our toddler! Thanks for your thoughtful gift. I know we'll be using it for years to come.

All my love,

Tanisha

Potty

Dear Gina,

Thank you so much for coming to our baby shower and for the potty with its training videos. It's such a great gift, and I loved your idea of putting one in the back of our SUV for "on the road" emergencies. It was nice to catch up, and I hope to get together again before the baby arrives. Thanks again for your thoughtful gift.

Sincerely,

Jacqueline

Prenatal Gift Basket

Dear Lorraine,

It was extremely thoughtful of you to put together a care package of prenatal essentials, especially as I enter my last trimester of my pregnancy. You're going to have to tell me where you found the anti-stretch cream. I'm going to use a tube a week at the rate I'm growing! The aromatherapy candles and bath salts are absolutely wonderful, and I'm looking forward to soaking away in a nice warm bath. Thanks again for all the prenatal goodies and for sharing in my special day.

Fondly,

Daisy

Prenatal Massage

Dear Jane,

Thank you so much for coming to my baby shower and for your decadent gift. I'm totally looking forward to my prenatal massage and having my little aches and pains disappear—at least for a little while! I'll let you know when I'm ready to schedule my appointment; maybe you can join me for an afternoon at the spa. It was extremely considerate of you to think of me and pick out the perfect "mommy" gift. Thanks again for everything.

Warmly,

Noreen

Quilt

Dear Mary,

Words can't express how I felt when I opened your baby gift. I still can't believe that you took the time to make such a lovely quilt for our new baby. You chose the most beautiful colors and softest fabric that I'm a little hesitant to put it to its intended use. Please don't be surprised if the next time you visit you see it on display in our living room! Thank you for taking the time to make such a personal gift – it's an absolute treasure.

With love,

Denise

Quilt Clips

Dear Laney,

Thank you so much for the hand-painted flower quilt clips. We received a lovely quilt for the baby and the quilt clips will be perfect to display it on the wall near baby's crib. Thanks again for coming to my baby shower, for the lovely gift, and for staying late to help clean up. You're a great friend.

Warmly,

Therese

Receiving Blanket

Dear Lois,

You've absolutely spoiled our new baby with your gift bag filled with receiving blankets, burp cloths, and the cute little trinket items. The blankets look so cozy, baby is sure to get a good night's sleep swaddled in something so comfy. It was very thoughtful of you to put together a care package of so many items. Thank you very much.

Fondly,

Kathy

Rocking Chair & Ottoman

Dear Mom and Dad,

Thank you so much for offering to buy us the rocking chair and ottoman that we saw at the store today. It's so comfortable, and the blue jean fabric on the white frame is perfect for the baby's room. It's incredible to think that we are soon to be parents, and we are so grateful to have your support during this very exciting time in our lives.

Love,

Noreen and Scott

Scrapbook

Dear Sheila,

Thank you so much for the scrapbook, newborn baby stickers, and patterned papers. I have wanted to learn how to get started but didn't know where to begin. The materials you gave me are perfect, and the magazine you've included has some really great ideas. Thanks again for getting me started on a fun new hobby!

Fondly,

Rebecca

Sling Carrier

Dear Cara,

Thanks for the cool baby gift! I absolutely love the sling carrier and am really excited to be able to carry baby close to me. I've seen moms using the sling at the mall, and it really looks like an easy way to tote baby when I need to run those quick errands and don't want to hassle with the stroller. Many thanks again.

Fondly,

Kimberly

Stock/Savings Certificate

Dear Uncle Bill,

What a fantastic surprise to receive a savings certificate for our new baby! We plan to open an educational savings plan for Ernie and start saving for his college expenses, so we appreciate your inaugural deposit. Of course, we'll have to find a second use for it if he gets a scholarship to play basketball! Thanks for your extremely thoughtful gift.

Love,

Dee and Sam

Stroller

Dear Grandma,

I was absolutely taken aback when we received the wonderful stroller you had shipped to us. I was so excited to share the news of our pregnancy with you last month but was not expecting to receive anything – at least not yet! It's apparent you did your research, too; this one looks like it could walk the baby for me. Sean and I thank you for your most generous gift and for always being so thoughtful. We love you and will call you soon to chat.

Love,

Elsa

Stroller (double/twin)

Dear Gloria and Chuck,

Thank you so much for your thoughtful gift. The twin stroller is absolutely perfect, and we especially like that the twins will be seated next to each other when they're out and about. I'm not sure I'll be ready for more than a daily walk to the park, so you can be sure the stroller will be put to a lot of good use. Thanks again for your thoughtful and extremely generous gift.

Love,

Kerry and Kyle

Stroller Activity Set

Dear Amy,

Thanks for the cute stroller attachment that has so many fun little detachable animals and sea creatures. I plan to take the baby on many walks, and this activity set is sure to keep baby amused along the way. I also love that it attaches to the car seat to ensure an entertaining ride wherever we go. Thanks again for the gift.

Fondly,

Jeanie

Stuffed Animal

Dear Jo,

Thank you for the cuddly teddy bear for baby. It's so adorable – it's hard not to play with it. I have a feeling Teddy will quickly become a baby favorite, and I won't be surprised if he even travels to college in 18 years! Thanks again for thinking of us.

Warmly,

Jennifer

Table/Night Stand

Dear Brenda,

Thank you for your lovely baby gift! It was very thoughtful of you to pick out a little nightstand to put next to the rocking chair in her room. I knew I needed something where I could place books and bottles, and the nightstand is perfect. I love the extra drawer space, too, and plan to store extra blankets in case it gets chilly during those late night feedings. Many thanks again for your thoughtful and generous gift.

Love,

Robin

Teething Blanket

Dear Bethany,

Your teething blanket, bib, and toys are a must-have for any mom, and I appreciate receiving your gift. I know that I'll have a teething baby soon enough, and now I feel prepared to handle baby's sore gums. Thanks again for coming to the baby shower and for your thoughtful gift.

Fondly,

Lindsay

Towel & Bath Items

Dear Terri,

Thank you for the two sets of hooded towels and matching washcloths. They are so soft! They are sure to keep baby warm and dry after bath or pool time. The little embroidered animals are adorable. I loved that you picked out something that will fit a little girl or boy. Only a few more weeks 'til we find out! Many thanks again.

Warmly,

Gina

Toys

Dear Laila,

Thank you for the sparkly aquarium crib toy. It plays such lovely music, it's sure to lull baby to sleep every night. I'm hoping the little action buttons will give her something to tinker around with in the morning and maybe give us a few extra minutes of sleep ...the best gift of all! All our thanks.

Warmly,

Jen and Joe

Tub Side Seat

Dear Jamie,

Thank you so much for the tub side seat. I'm grateful I won't have to lean over our deep tub at bath time, and the extra storage space is going to be a perfect place to store tub toys. Before we know it, baby will be stepping on it to wash his hands after potty time! Thanks for the very useful and thoughtful gift.

Sincerely,

Suzanne

Unfamiliar item

Dear Aunt Sally,

Thank you for the yellow and green pocketed-pouch. What a unique item! We plan to use it in the bathroom to hold all of baby's bath items and toys in one convenient place. Thank you for your thoughtful and original gift.

Fondly,

Rebecca

Volunteer Time

Dear Caryn,

Just a quick note to thank you for all your help in getting the baby's room ready, for the meal's you've prepared, and for helping out whenever I've called. I really appreciate your time and devotion to helping us during this very exciting time, and I am very grateful for your friendship. I wanted to make sure you knew how much we love and appreciate you!

Love,

Dena and Sean

Wipe Warmer

Dear Yvonne,

On behalf of baby, thank you for the wipe warmer! I could never be so cruel to use a cool wipe on a warm baby bottom and appreciate your gift and the box of wipes. Thanks again for coming to my shower and for your thoughtful gift.

Fondly,

Kay

Chapter Four

Notes for Special People

The success of your baby shower may depend on the help of many people, and they each deserve a special thank you note for their time and effort to ensure you had a lovely day. While it may be one person who coordinated the whole event at their home or several co-workers who shared the responsibility, it's important to recognize each of them with a personal thank you note for their role in coordinating your shower.

Giving Your Hostess a Gift

It's customary to give your host(s) a token thank you gift, which can range from a bouquet of fresh flowers, personalized stationery or a gift certificate for a manicure at the local spa. The size of the shower may determine your gift and should always include a personalized thank you note recognizing her for her time and effort.

In the event several friends hosted the shower, it's appropriate to give the same gift if the responsibility was equally shared, but be sure to personalize each note and acknowledge each one separately for something they did individually. Give the host(s) her thank you gift when she has a free moment on the day of your shower. Some popular times are before all the guests arrive, when everyone is eating (accompanied by a little presentation by you), or after the guests have departed.

Ideally, the host(s) thank you note and gift should be given on the day of the shower. In the event your host also gave you a gift, send a note for the present and thank her again for the shower. If your shower happened and you still need to give a note and hostess gift, be sure to make this the first one delivered. You certainly don't want to upset your host if she finds out others have received thank you notes when she has yet to receive hers.

Sample Notes to the Host(s) of Your Baby Shower

When writing your notes, be sure to appropriately acknowledge the host's role in coordinating your shower.

Hostess Thank You

Dear Christina,

Thank you so much for hosting a lovely baby shower at your beautiful home. You've completely outdone yourself. You made me feel like a princess for a day! I truly appreciate all of your hard work, from picking out the cutest invitations to making a delicious buffet lunch and coordinating the fun games. Many thanks again for your generosity in hosting this special day.

Love,

Candy

If several friends united to host your shower, try to acknowledge their specific role in coordinating your party.

Hostess Thank You

Dear Elizabeth,

I just wanted to share how much I appreciated everything you did to ensure I had a wonderful baby shower. I especially loved all of the decorations you picked out to match our baby bedding. I noticed all of the baby "wild animals" throughout the house! The whole day was quite lovely. I only wish we had more time to chat, and I hope you'll be free one day soon to help me organize all the thoughtful gifts we received. Many thanks again for helping to coordinate such a memorable day.

Love,

Tanya

Dear Suzie,

I hope you're not tired of my thank you notes, but I had to let you know how much I love the cute clothes and sleepers you picked out for our new baby. The little sleepers look super cozy, and I hope they'll help baby get a good night sleep. You've absolutely spoiled the baby and me with your participation in hosting a baby shower and with your gifts. I can't wait for the opportunity to reciprocate! Thanks again for everything.

Love,

Tracy

Host of Your Office Shower

There are a few situations that may precede an office shower, and it's up to you to find out who coordinated your shower and who was financially responsible for it. In the event the department manager or the company paid for the shower, a thank you note must be sent to the manager thanking her for the lovely shower. Or if several people each contributed money for the shower, you should send notes to the key coordinators. Many times, staff in one's department may each pitch in for lunch and a group gift, in which case a note should be sent to the primary coordinator who should be asked to share your thanks with the rest of the group. Some examples of each of these scenarios follow.

A Note to the Boss

Dear Melissa,

It was extremely generous of you and the ABC Company to host a baby shower in honor of our expected baby. I was extremely surprised by the care you took in planning such a lovely luncheon, and truly enjoyed sharing in the excitement of our baby with my friends and fellow staff. Thank you also for the high chair, booster seat, embroidered bibs, and all the clothes and toys. You can be sure everything will be put to good use in the coming year!

I am very lucky to have you as my employer and appreciate all that you've done. Thanks again for the lovely shower.

Sincerely,

Meghan

Dear Trudy,

It was extremely generous of you and the finance team to host a baby shower and spoil our little Smith with all the gifts. I was very surprised to come to the "meeting" and find everyone there ready to party! The Mexican food was great, and it was a hoot to play some of the wildest baby shower games ever – with the guys! Steve and I really appreciate all your hard work and hope you will share our thanks with everyone else in the office. Many thanks again for the fun lunch, great gifts, and all the well wishes as we wait for baby to join us.

Sincerely,

Trina

Group Coordinated Effort

Dear Bianca,

Mark and I would like to thank you and the staff of the Marketing Department for the lovely luncheon in honor of our expected baby. I was so taken aback by everyone's warm wishes and generosity in picking out such lovely and much needed gifts as we await the arrival of baby. As I'm now on maternity leave, I hope you will share my thanks with the entire team and please let everyone know how much we appreciated the party.

Baby is due in just a few weeks, and I'll be sure to email photos as soon as possible. Thanks again for everything.

Sincerely,

Bonnie

Chapter Five

Notes for Unique Situations

Unless you're expecting triplets, you may not need three baby carriers, or maybe you received a bedding ensemble you didn't register for and clearly do not want. This section provides detailed examples of how to acknowledge unique situations, such as receiving duplicate gifts, gifts you do not want, and broken or damaged items. These situations occur and must be handled candidly, without embarrassing the gift giver or yourself.

Receiving Duplicate Gifts

There are several reasons why you may receive duplicate items. Thanks to convenient store policies, returning gifts is often easy. When you receive duplicate presents at your baby shower, immediately thank each gift giver for her thoughtfulness. The givers will know you have to return a duplicate, and usually someone will give you the gift receipt for the exchange.

When sending the thank you note, do not mention that the gift was a duplicate. Thank the giver for their thoughtful and generous gift as if it was the only one you received.

Receiving Something You Do Not Want

You may have a friend who chose to buy a gift without looking at your registry. When opening the gift at your shower, it's always best to show your appreciation and find something nice to say about the item. If someone who isn't expected to visit gave the gift, send a thank you note as if you plan to put the gift to its intended use. If, on the other hand, it's a family member or close friend who is sure to visit when the baby is born, let them know before their visit that you exchanged the item and why.

Returned Item

Dear Aunt Mae,

Thank you so much for the Noah's Ark lamp, nightlight, and switch plate cover. We completed setting up the baby's room last month, and we had already purchased a set that matches the bedding. The ensemble you picked out is very nice, and I hope you don't mind that we exchanged it for lovely lavender and white polka dot curtains we've had our eyes on. They look beautiful in the baby's room, and I can't wait to have you over to see them! Every time we look out the sunny windows, we will remember you and your generous gift. Many thanks again.

Love,

Aimee and Paul

Receiving an Unwanted Gift Without a Receipt

     Occasionally you may receive an item you do not want, and the gift giver did not include a gift receipt. These situations are delicate and should be handled according to your relationship with the gift giver. If it was a close family member or friend, it's appropriate to let them know you would like to exchange the gift for something else and ask if they received a gift receipt that you could use. If they don't have a receipt, hopefully you can find out where they bought the gift and you may still be able to exchange the item or receive credit for a future purchase. Thank the gift giver appropriately, as described above, especially if you already discussed your future return of their item.

     If it was a casual friend or acquaintance who gave you the gift, etiquette allows you to ask your close friends if they know where the item was purchased. If it was an inexpensive item, like clothes for example, it is not recommended that you contact the person for the receipt. You should send a thank you note as if you plan to put it to its intended use, then find a second home for the gift or set it aside for another occasion. If it is an expensive item, it is recommended that after you send your thank you note, you call the person and thank them again, but let them know your need for wanting to exchange the item. Handle the call with care, and you may then find out if they have a receipt or if you can have the name of the store.

Receiving a Broken or Damaged Gift

With the advent of the Internet, registry shopping has never been easier, including having items shipped directly to your home. Occasionally, however, something may arrive broken or damaged, in which case the receipt or shipping invoice should offer detailed instructions on how to return the item. The store will usually ship a new item upon notification, in which case you should send a thank you note upon the gift's arrival, without mentioning that it arrived broken.

However, if your friend self-packed an item that arrived broken, etiquette suggests that you do not mention the damage to prevent the sender from feeling obliged to spend additional time and money on a new baby gift. If the package was insured, a label will provide you with detailed instructions on how to recover the gift's value from the shipping company.

Damaged or Broken Gift

Dear Ally,

Thank you so much for the lovely Christening outfit you made for the baby. The dress and head piece are absolutely beautiful, and I especially love the glass beads you wove into the trim. Knowing the time and great care you put into making it, I was upset when the package arrived damaged. The dress was a little torn and had a big watermark on the front. It was extremely thoughtful of you to insure the package, and I notified the post office of the damage. They'll send you a claim form with directions on how to complete the claim. I've already taken the dress to a wonderful seamstress who has promised to return it fully repaired and cleaned. I hope you're not upset by the damage. It was extremely thoughtful of you to make such a precious dress, and I can't wait for you to see the baby wear it on her special day.

Love,

Lori

Appendix A: Sample Gift List

Maintain one gift list of all the items you received for baby. This includes gifts from the baby shower, items received in the mail, and presents from friends who dropped by.

Name	Address	Gift	Thank You Note
Sherri & Tom Casarrana	90552 W. Fontaine St. Anywhere, USA 00000	Crib & mattress	5/31/05
Jan & Bill Riley	123 Alpha St. Anywhere, USA 00000	Two sleepers	7/15/05

Appendix B: Sample Baby Registry

This sample registry will help you identify all of the items you may need in anticipation of baby's arrival.

Item	Style
Artwork	
Baby Gate	
Baby Proofing Items	
Backpack Carrier	
Bassinet	
Bath Towels	
Bath Toys	
Bath Tub	
Bedding Set	
Blankets	
Books	
Booster Seat	
Boppy Pillow	
Bottles	
Bottle Sterilizer	
Bottle Warmer	
Bouncer	
Bouncy Seat	
Breast Pump	
Burp Cloths	
Car Seat	
Carrier	
CD Player	
Changing Pad	

Changing Pad Cover	
Changing Table	
Cloth Diapers	
Clothes	
Cradle Swing	
Crib	
Crib Bumpers	
Crib Sheets	
Decorations	
Diaper Bag	
Diaper Trashcan	
Diapers	
Drapes/Curtains	
DVDs & Videos	
Formula	
Frames	
Gift Card	
Hamper	
Health Care Kit	
High Chair	
Humidifier	
Jogging Stroller	
Jumper	
Mattress	
Mobile	
Monitor – Audio	
Monitor – Video	
Music	
Pack 'N Play	
Personalized Items	
Photo Album	

Play Mat/Gym	
Play Saucer	
Play Yard	
Potty	
Quilt	
Quilt Clips	
Receiving Blankets	
Rocking Chair	
Scrapbook	
Sling Carrier	
Storage Baskets	
Stroller	
Stroller Activity Set	
Stuffed Animals	
Table/Night Stand	
Teething Blanket	
Toys	
Tub Side Seat	
Washcloths	
Wipe Warmer	

Notes:

Index